T0027389

HANSEL & GRETEL

Kneehigh's
HANSEL & GRETEL
Written by Carl Grose

methuen | drama
LONDON · NEW YORK · OXFORD · NEW DELHI · SYDNEY

METHUEN DRAMA
Bloomsbury Publishing Plc
50 Bedford Square, London, WC1B 3DP, UK
1385 Broadway, New York, NY 10018, USA
29 Earlsfort Terrace, Dublin 2, Ireland

BLOOMSBURY, METHUEN DRAMA and the Methuen Drama logo
are trademarks of Bloomsbury Publishing Plc

First published in Great Britain by Oberon Books 2010
This edition published by Methuen Drama 2023

Copyright © Carl Grose, 2010

Carl Grose has asserted his right under the Copyright,
Designs and Patents Act, 1988, to be identified as author of this work.

All rights reserved. No part of this publication may be reproduced or
transmitted in any form or by any means, electronic or mechanical,
including photocopying, recording, or any information storage or retrieval
system, without prior permission in writing from the publishers.

Bloomsbury Publishing Plc does not have any control over, or responsibility for,
any third-party websites referred to or in this book. All internet addresses given
in this book were correct at the time of going to press. The author and publisher
regret any inconvenience caused if addresses have changed or sites have
ceased to exist, but can accept no responsibility for any such changes.

All rights whatsoever in this play are strictly reserved and application for performance etc.
should be made before rehearsals by professionals and by amateurs to Julia Kreitman,
The Agency (London) Ltd., 24 Pottery Lane, Holland Park, London W11 4LZ.
No performance may be given unless a licence has been obtained.

A catalogue record for this book is available from the British Library.

ISBN: PB: 978-1-3504-6125-3
eBook: 978-1-8494-3731-8

Series: Modern Plays

Printed and bound in Great Britain

To find out more about our authors and books visit www.bloomsbury.com
and sign up for our newsletters.

Kneehigh

Kneehigh are a Cornwall-based theatre company with a local, national and international profile. For over 30 years we have created vigorous, popular and challenging theatre, performing with joyful anarchy.

We tell stories. Based in breath-taking barns on the south coast, we create theatre of humanity on an epic and tiny scale. We work with an ever changing ensemble of performers, artists and musicians, and are passionate about our multi-disciplined creative process.

In 2010, we launched the Asylum, a beautiful and flexible nomadic structure, which means we now have a venue to call home, as well as remaining one of the leading touring theatre companies in the UK. We have now presented six seasons in the Asylum in Cornwall, and will continue to reinvent the space and explore new locations in future years.

Alongside our national and international touring and Asylum seasons, we run the Kneehigh Rambles, aiming to engage creatively with communities in Cornwall and beyond through event and adventure.

Hansel & Gretel was first performed on the 4th December 2009 at Bristol Old Vic and was a co-production between Kneehigh and Bristol Old Vic. The original cast was as follows:

GRETEL, Joanna Holden

HANSEL, Craig Johnson

FATHER, The Witch, Carl Grose

MOTHER, The Bird, Giles King

MUSICIAN/JACOB, Stu Barker

MUSICIAN/WILHELM, Ian Ross

STAGE MANAGER/ANIMATOR, Fay Powell-Thomas

Hansel & Gretel was revived and opened at Warwick Arts Centre on 26th November, 2010, and played at the QEH Theatre on the South Bank, London, with the following cast:

GRETEL, Joanna Holden

HANSEL, Chris Price

FATHER/ THE WITCH, Carl Grose

MOTHER/ THE BIRD, Edith Tankus

MUSICIAN/JACOB, TJ Holmes

MUSICIAN/WILHELM, Benji Bower

STAGE MANAGER/ANIMATOR, Fay Powell-Thomas

Hansel & Gretel Creative & Production Team

Director, Mike Shepherd

Writer, Carl Grose

Musical Director, Ian Ross

Co-Composers, Stu Barker & Ian Ross

Designer, Michael Vale

Lighting Designer, Mike Gunning

Sound Designer, Jason Barnes

Puppetry Consultant, Sarah Wright

Mechanical Sculptor, Rob Higgs

Choreographer, Emma Rice

Assistant Director, Simon Harvey

Producer, Paul Crewes

Production Manager, David Harraway

Lighting Operator, Ben Nichols/Liam Cleary (revival)

Sound Operator, Sally Evans/Phil Innes (revival)

Wardrobe/Props, Ruth Shepherd

Props, Laura McKenzie

Set Construction, Bristol Old Vic

Puppet Makers, Lyndie Wright, Geraldine Spiller, Sarah Wright

For Kneehigh:

Executive Producer, Ali Robertson
Artistic Director, Mike Shepherd
General Manager, Charlotte Bond
Producer, Liz King
Company Stage Manager, Steph Curtis
Technical Stage Manager, Aled William Thomas
Finance Officer, Fiona Buxton
Development Officer, Bethany Lyne
Communications Assistant, Dann Carroll
Production Assistant, Millie Jones
Rambles Lead Artist, Anna Maria Murphy
Marketing, Sam McAuley & Kym Bartlett
Press, Clióna Roberts
Photography, Steve Tanner
Film Maker, Brett Harvey
Illustrator, Daryl Waller

Kneehigh Board:
Alan Livingston (Chair), Peter Cox, Teresa Gleadowe, Sheila Healy, Clare Morpurgo, Daphne Skinnard, Simon Williams

Revered Accomplices:
Emma Rice & Paul Crewes

Kneehigh Associate Artists:
Simon Baker, Stu Barker, Carl Grose, Simon Harvey, Charles Hazlewood, Etta Murfitt, Anna Maria Murphy, Malcolm Rippeth, Steve Tanner, Ian Ross, Daryl Waller, Sarah Wright

Kneehigh Cookbook:

We are often asked how we make our shows. We've created a brand new members' website, the Kneehigh Cookbook, which is crammed full of exclusive videos, documents, pictures and plans about how and why we make our work.

You can sample the inspiration for our shows, graze in the performing section, hear Emma Rice talk about casting or Mike Shepherd discuss improvisation.

The Cookbook is free for everyone to use, and you can sign up today at kneehighcookbook.co.uk.

The Chicken Takes The Elevator:
Making Kneehigh's *Hansel & Gretel*

The question is often asked: "How do you make a Kneehigh show?"

Truth is, I'm never quite sure how to answer that. I believe it's about the people. The right combination of artists who adventure to tell a story that feels right; a story that *has* to be told. But then, that isn't a very helpful answer. People, particularly students, often want specifics. And fair enough.

So, I've remembered one – an important moment, personal to me, in the making of our production of *Hansel & Gretel* that stands as a defining example Kneehigh's creative process, albeit in microcosm.

It goes something like this...

In the show, we had two plump puppet chickens named Diane and Maureen. During rehearsals, Craig Johnson and myself were tasked with a problem by our director, Mike Shepherd: How can we get these two weighty flightless birds up onto a stool so that the scene (and the story) might continue? Craig, a brilliant puppeteer, conjured an improvised, virtuoso sequence before our eyes whereby his chicken, Diane (named after his mum), performed a laborious but seriously funny "rock climb" up the side of the stool using her beak and the momentum from her body to scale its heights. It was a sensation. Mike was pleased. Then... it was our turn. Maureen and me. We were both nervous and annoyed. How could we ever follow that? Or, in the spirit of friendly competition, better it? To confess it now (though of course, we didn't dare show it at the time), Maureen and I had nothing... no ideas, no skills, no hope of topping Craig and Diane's genius... and so we prepared to enter... the Arena of Failure. However, let me share with you something that most drama handbooks never usually talk about: skirting the edge of failure is *the* most exciting place to be – not just in rehearsals but in any creative endeavor! For in that moment of having zero "brilliant ideas", in the very moment of letting go, Maureen, despondent, pecked a "button" (which wasn't there) on the side of the stool... and took the elevator! So I thought quickly and provided hydraulic sound effects. Maureen reached the top. Joined her friend. I was saved from losing face in the rehearsal room. Mike was in stitches. The moment was "in". Even Craig was forced to concede it worked. Hoorah!

The chicken had taken the elevator.

The process of "making" a show is one of freedom and playfulness. However, that isn't to say the work in a Kneehigh rehearsal space is random, slapdash, or without rigor. Quite the reverse. Mike Shepherd and myself (along with composers and designers) will spend long periods of pre-rehearsal time (years, sometimes) talking about the story – why we like it, why it feels relevant to now, and how we might tell it. Then I write. A structure. Scenes. Lyrics. It becomes a script. But that in itself is also informed by workshop discoveries (the rabbit narrators in the script you're holding now came out of Giles King playing (there's that word again) around with some old manky bunny puppets Mike had found) Set design ideas are also fed into creative discussion early, as does the current state of the world around us...

In rehearsals, I write the script again as each scene is put on its feet, strengthening language and shape. Mike selects and edits devised offers – a vital skill in work such as this. Everyone is thinking about the story. Everyone is back and forth with play and rigor. Everyone is seeking to discover what feels *right*. Nerves are held. Once the show has opened before an audience, it is worked on still. Continuously. Sometimes without end.

Indeed, it could be said that a show is never truly finished. Never truly perfect. And why would you want it to be? Theatre *should* be imperfect, existing in the moment, uncertain, exciting, dangerous, hilarious and alive.

Hansel & Gretel is a collaboration between many people. It is my hope that this script gives a vivid taste of all the elements used in the show, from Michael Vale's skeletal wood-and-rust set, to Ian Ross and Stu Barker's brilliantly eerie, witty folk music; from Rob Higgs' fabulous contraptions (yes, they all actually work) to

Geraldine Spiller, Lyndie and Sarah Wright's charming puppets; from Mike Shepherd's inspired rough "wonder tale" take on the story (you'll find no sickly-sweet candy-cane house here), to the touching and deranged characters created by the performers. It is hoped that this script in some small way reveals a rough blueprint for a show that was ever changing, ever evolving, and ever present in that magic moment of play, rigor, and fabulous unknowing.

Long may the chicken take the elevator.

Play on!

Carl Grose

Writer of *Hansel & Gretel*

On Making Theatre:
Some Thoughts from Director Mike Shepherd

When I first look at a story my starting point is often – "that bit's not very good how can I make it better?" rather than "that's brilliant!" So a creative process can start from adversity as well as inspiration.

For me, there was plenty in *Hansel & Gretel* to make better – ditch the lame white dove, make the witch's dim-witted demise much more exciting, and make Gretel more than just Hansel's weedy tag-along sister. In fact, one of the first decisions was to make Gretel very feisty and ingenious – so she became an engineer and an inventor.

At the same time as I was thinking about this story, I happened to hear about a brilliant young inventor and engineer who had moved to Cornwall, bought a sunken fishing boat for £50, refloated it and lived on it. I Googled him and found he specialized in brilliant and quirky chain reaction contraptions. His name was Rob Higgs. More on him later…

And so to the Kneehigh barns (our creative space in Cornwall) for an R&D (research and development) period – this is vital time spent discovering elements of the show before rehearsals begin. There, we muster a "toolkit" to explore what the show might become – there's costume, random props, music etc – a living, changing catalogue of potential.

Often the creative space is overlooked in the creative process – rehearsal rooms can often be stark, windowless environments devoid of atmosphere. The barns are situated quite literally on the Cornish cliffs. They let the weather in and out. We make fires. We cook together. And we focus intensively on the work while we're there.

We don't rehearse in the R&Ds, but tackle the story's grand moments with broad brushstrokes using whatever's to hand. Here's where the brilliant Rob Higgs comes in again… During one session, we attempted to give ourselves a day to explore the final scene involving The Witch stoking her flames in readiness to cook Hansel. We knew that The Witch was tending to a fire-pit, that Hansel was suspended in a cage, and that Gretel was deemed too dangerous to be free and was tied to a chair... Rob Higgs was tasked to create a chain reaction in a limited amount of time using whatever he could find, which resulted in Hansel being sprung from his caged position to swing across the fire and to eventually collide with The Witch and thus knocking her into the flames. I brought a bunch of locals up to witness this attempt at the final denouement. It looked exciting. Dangerous, even. And it was. But there was cheering when the contraption snapped, Hansel swung, and the Witch met her end. So it obviously worked.

Because I prefer to act and probably because I quickly tire of negotiating the often vulnerable nature of actors' egos I am often a reluctant director, but I strongly believe that a switched-on strong director is vital for this kind of playful and crafted work.

Let me describe a simple scene where mother, starving, fights a puppet chicken for a worm, eats the worm and in despair turns to her husband and says "I've eaten a worm...oh I miss our children!" There was a period in the tour when I didn't see the show for three weeks, but when I returned Mother (brilliantly played by Giles King) and the worm had developed bizarrely, edging the scene off into some other realm. Mother conjured a multitude of worms from the ground with a bagpipe solo, the worms then ate her legs as she told her husband she was experiencing a phantom pregnancy! The scene was reined back in. With marvelously inventive actors like this you need a director so that the story doesn't spiral wildly into a parallel world!

So – with some sort of conclusion – start with a specific or two and ask "What If?". Fuel your creative space with the possibility, and through selecting, editing and craft find clarity from chaos!

Mike Shepherd
Director of *Hansel & Gretel*,
Founder of Kneehigh

Characters

HANSEL

GRETEL

MOTHER

FATHER

THE OLD LADY / THE WITCH / STRANGER IN THE WOODS

BIRDY
A familiar

JACOB & WILHELM
Musical neighbours from across the valley

RABBITS

DIANE & MAUREEN
Chickens

GRAHAM
A ferret

ACT ONE

The SUPERNATURE CHORUS emerge from the shadows. They wear Tyrolean hats, capes and laderhosen. They sing:

SONG
Once upon a time
When suns were trusted to shine
And birds, they sang the songs of May
A saying was often spoke of this way -
Take each day as it comes
Take each day as it comes
Take each day as it comes
Take each day as it comes...

Two RABBITS appear. They sing along, nibble at the ground, etc.

RABBIT 1: I like grass.

RABBIT 2: Me too. It's sweet.

They nibble grass.

RABBIT 2: I've never been this far from home before...

RABBIT 1: This is where the woodcutter and his family live.

Here we find a home made of ramshackle things – rope, planks, pots and assorted useful junk lies scattered about.

SONG
Once upon a time
When rivers met up with the tide
And winds, they blew a happier tune
And dusk it hid from the light of the moon
Take each day as it comes
Take each day as it comes
Take each day as it comes
Take each day as it comes...

Enter HANSEL & GRETEL. Our heroes. They have a tinkle in their eyes.

Above, a bird cries. They watch it circle. A feather tumbles down. GRETEL catches it, and tickles HANSEL.

RABBIT 1: That's Hansel & Gretel.

RABBIT 2: They're twins.

HANSEL & GRETEL sneeze simultaneously.

RABBIT 1: Identical!

RABBIT 2: *(Sniffs the air.)* I feel a bit frightened.

RABBIT 1: You must take each day as it comes. You never know what might happen.

SNAP! The sound of a rabbit snare echoes through the forest! They freeze and hammer their back feet on the ground, indicating immediate danger – bud-bud-bud-bud-bud – then vanish.

HANSEL: *(Reads his encyclopedia.)* Gretel, listen to this. It says here the universe is infinite, that it has no end… Imagine that!

GRETEL tickles HANSEL again.

Stop it! I'm trying to read my encyclopedia. *(Reads.)* Oh! Did you know that the deepest place in the ocean is 12 miles down? 12 miles…

GRETEL: *(Bored, sees –)* Hansel, look at that apple!

Indeed, there's a big red one suspended high above…

GRETEL: It's a beauty! Good enough to eat!

HANSEL: It's too high. We'll never reach it.

Determined, GRETEL fetches a huge plank.

HANSEL: *(Reading.)* Gretel, did you know that there are over 200 bones in the human body, half of which are in the hands and feet!

GRETEL: Right. I've listened to you read out yer facts and figures. Now you can help me with my engineering. Come on!

They spring into action, HANSEL following GRETEL's orders – collects various pieces of junk lying about – a lobster pot, bungee cord, the plank, a bouy on a rope. A contraption is assembled.

GRETEL: Hansel? Grab that! Put it there, in the middle. We'll use it as a fulcrum. This plank will act like a see-saw. Tie that on. Nice and tight! Find something of good weight to place on the end… there!

HANSEL places a bouy tied to a long piece of rope at one end of the plank.

Now brother, I want you to stand on that stool and on the count of three, I want you to jump!

HANSEL: Is this safe, Gretel?

GRETEL: Hansel, what could possibly go wrong? Ready?

HANSEL: Yes…

GRETEL: One, two, three – jump!

HANSEL jumps off the stool, onto the other end of the plank, which launches the bouy into the air. It hits the apple with perfect precision and falls into GRETEL's hands.

HANSEL: Ohhh, give us a bite!

HANSEL takes it off her. GRETEL tries to get it back.

GRETEL: Oi! That's mine!

HANSEL: Here you are…

> *(Snatches it away.)*

Can't have it!

> *(Offers it.)*

Here you are…

> *(Snatches it away.)*

Can't have it!

> *(Offers it.)*

No, really, here you are. Can't have it!

> *GRETEL punches him in the stomach and takes the apple. She takes a bite and gives us a wink.*

FATHER: Timber!

> *A tree crashes through the air. They expertly duck.*

FATHER: *(Holding an axe aloft.)* Good morning, children!

HANSEL & GRETEL: Good morning, father!

FATHER: What a beautiful day!

MOTHER: *(Holding a dead rabbit aloft.)* Good morning, children!

HANSEL & GRETEL: Good morning, mother!

MOTHER: Rabbit pie for tea!

> *A flurry of activity as we see the family in their element – happy, noisy, full of life. Music accompanies as –*

> *GRETEL & MOTHER skin the rabbit behind as FATHER circles with a barrow full of wood. He sets up a chopping block…*

FATHER: Hansel, my boy, put that damned encyclopedia down for one moment, will ya? I think it's high time I taught you how to chop wood. But first, let's test your strength – fight me, boy.

Hand in hand, they prepare to fight –

FATHER & HANSEL: One, two, three, four
I declare thumb war
Bow, kiss… bow, kiss… bow, kiss!

A game of Thumb War ensues. FATHER allows himself to be beaten. HANSEL gets carried away…

FATHER: Well done, boy! You are strong! Come! Meet your log!

HANSEL: Hello Mr. Log!

FATHER: Don't get too attached.

HANSEL: Goodbye Mr. Log.

FATHER: Observe the way the lines in the wood run?

HANSEL: Is that called "The Grain", Father?

FATHER: Is it, my boy. Having your nose stuck in that book is paying off! Now you want to chop *with* the grain, never against it –

HANSEL: Father? Will this wood-chopping lesson put me on the right path to becoming… a man?

FATHER: Oh, I hope so, son. I hope so.

HANSEL: "With the grain, not against it." Continue.

FATHER offers his axe to HANSEL as MOTHER & GRETEL take the focus – they skin the rabbit!

MOTHER: That's it darling. Cut around the throat. Now, remove the skin. Now, yank it! Yank it!

GRETEL: Like this, mother?

FATHER: That's it, Hansel. Take a good strong stance! Now, picture yourself as the axe blade – keen and sharp and glinty – see the target, lift high and –

HANSEL chops the wood as GRETEL skins the rabbit. Everyone cheers.

21

MOTHER: Oh well done, darling! One skinned rabbit ready for the pot!

FATHER: Congratulations, Hansel! Your first piece of kindling!

HANSEL: Father, was I a tree once?

FATHER: What on earth are you talking about?

HANSEL: It's in my encyclopedia. It says here that the Hindus believe in the concept of reincarnation. They say in a previous life you were something else entirely! I wondered if perhaps I was once a tree, and if it hurt when I was chopped into kindling…?

FATHER: Oh Hansel, you're so clever yer daft. Come on, boy. Let's go get a beer!

They go off. MOTHER hangs up a washing line.

MOTHER: NOW, where are those flapping chickens?

Two plump CHICKENS run in from the back. They are DIANE and MAUREEN. They have difficulty getting up onto the chopping block stool. However, DIANE manages to use her rock climbing skills. MAUREEN, meanwhile, takes the elevator.

MOTHER: Now, let's see what they've got for us today, eh Gretel?

GRETEL pops three eggs from the chickens.

Not a bad batch, you clucking hens, but you'd best keep this up or else… chop! chop!

DIANE and MAUREEN fly into a blind panic and go.

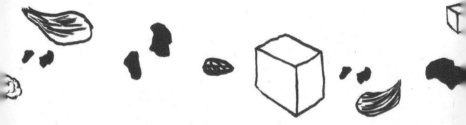

MOTHER: Feed them up, Gretel. Then you can lock them up in the hen house for the night.

GRETEL: Feed the chickens. *(Idea!)* Right.

Enter FATHER & HANSEL.

FATHER: *(A strange high-pitched call.)* Graham?

HANSEL: *(Loud, trying to mimick.)* Graham?

FATHER: Graham?

HANSEL: Graaaham?

FATHER: Graham!

HANSEL: Graham!

FATHER: Hansel m'boy, I think it's high time I taught you the homing call of Graham The Ferret. Now he's out there in the forest, foraging for fruit and nuts – but we must call him home. Observe my boy, assume the position, and summon him thus –

FATHER makes the call. (Note: it should be suitably bizarre and impossible to repeat and should ideally be different every time the line is performed.)

Now you try m'boy.

HANSEL tries calling him but can't do it.

FATHER: Not bad. But let's try it together! Father and son.

They call together.

FATHER: Oh look! Here he comes, Hansel! That's it, Graham! Look at him, Hansel, he's full of the joys of spring!

A FERRET scampers across the yard and up FATHER's leg into his lederhosen.

FATHER: Home sweet home, eh Graham? Oh, he's frisky today, Hansel!

HANSEL: Father? Will I have a ferret in my trousers one day?

FATHER: I'm sure you will, son. I'm sure you will…

HANSEL: Yes!

He goes off. MOTHER appears and repeats the Call of the Wild.

MOTHER: Oh, husband. I remember the first time you called for your ferret. You still know how to impress a woman.

FATHER: Even after all these years, wife?

MOTHER: What woman would tire of the old ferret-up-the trouser trick?

FATHER: Oh, babooshska.

MOTHER: Dance with me.

They dance romantically. GRETEL enters with a large metal contraption strapped to her.

GRETEL: Mother? Father? My new invention!

MOTHER: Whatever is it, darling?

GRETEL: It's an auto-rotating bucket-winch chicken feeder!

MOTHER: What does it do?

GRETEL: I'll show ya.

She fires it up.

FATHER: Take cover!

THE PARENTS run as GRETEL actives her machine – it fires corn like bullets! The CHICKENS appear and gobble it all up.

GRETEL: Plump, happy, egg-laying chickens!

MOTHER: Oh well done, sweetheart! Careful now, or you'll be pecked to death!

MOTHER & GRETEL go off.

The CHICKENS get up onto the chopping block again (this time, they both use the elevator).

DIANE: Oh, Maureen.

MAUREEN: Oh, Diane.

DIANE: What a feast that was!

MAUREEN: I feel fit to burst, I really do.

DIANE: What a time of plenty we do live in.

MAUREEN: Mm… I feel like I'm living in Hen Heaven.

DIANE: I feel like I'm living in Poultry Paradise.

MAUREEN: We're lucky to be with such a fine family, aren't we, Diane?

DIANE: Oh! We are, Maureen. They're kind, they're loving, and they look after their own. And just as long as we keep popping they eggs out –

MAUREEN/DIANE: Nuthin' can go wrong!

The distant sound of yodelling.

DIANE: 'ark!

MAUREEN: Is that who I think it is?

DIANE: I think it is!

MAUREEN: It's –

DIANE & MAUREEN: Jacob and Wilhelm!

Enter JACOB & WILHELM, two yodelling musicians.

MOTHER: Hello Jacob! Hello Wilhelm! Our musical neighbours from across the valley. Make yourselves at home, won't you boys?

JACOB: Thank you.

WILHELM: Thank you.

HANSEL: Gretel. A question: why do you think Mother's been busy in the kitchen baking?

GRETEL: Probably for the same reason Father's been busy wrapping presents!

HANSEL: Would that be the same reason he's been teaching me how to chop wood in readiness to become… a man?

GRETEL: And the same reason Jacob and Wilhelm are here with their special birthday instruments!

HANSEL: And what is that?

GRETEL: *(To us.)* Give him a minute or two.

> *HANSEL thinks. MOTHER & FATHER stand on the table with a big, lit birthday cake. JACOB & WILHELM play.*

HANSEL: Oh! It's our birthday!

> *GRETEL rolls her eyes.*

SONG
There is one unique day in every year
When we all raise a heartfelt cheer
No day puts us in finer fettle
So happy birthday Hansel
Happy birthday Gretel!

> *The PARENTS do a celebratory fireworks display (mimed).*

MOTHER & FATHER: Happy Birthday, children!

> *FATHER hands out presents.*

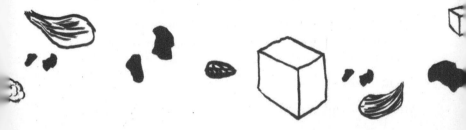

FATHER: Now this is for you and this is for you! Well, go on. Open them!

HANSEL & GRETEL tear open the presents – beautiful wood carved figures of themselves.

GRETEL: It's me!

HANSEL: It's me!

FATHER: I carved them myself.

MOTHER: Now blow out the candle, darlings, and make a wish! I wonder what this year will bring?

HANSEL & GRETEL blow… the atmosphere suddenly changes as FAMINE STRIKES. Howling wind! The cake vanishes! The washing line gets striped! Crows circle!

DIANE & MAUREEN, now scrawny, get blown in.

MAUREEN: Oh, Diane!

DIANE: Oh, Maureen… look at us!

MAUREEN: Skin and bone.

DIANE: What a year it's been, Maureen.

MAUREEN: A year of drought, Diane!

DIANE: A year of endless famine!

MAUREEN: Of vacant skies!

DIANE: Times are tough.

MAUREEN: Times are rough. You said this would happen, this blight upon the land.

DIANE: I saw omens, Maureen. Portents.

MAUREEN: Omens! Portents!

DIANE: I saw a buzzard flying backwards!

MAUREEN: I saw a snake swallow itself whole!

DIANE: I saw the moon fall out the sky!

MAUREEN: I saw the sun turn as black as sack-cloth.

DIANE: I saw a family of badgers singing Christmas carols – in July!

MAUREEN: Omens! Portents!

DIANE: I tell you, Maureen. This famine does nothing for egg production.

MAUREEN: Well get busy, Diane. For what good is a chicken who cannot lay?

MOTHER approaches.

MOTHER: Right you stubborn birds. Let's see if you've done any better today?

MAUREEN tries to lay but can't. DIANE pops out a small one.

MOTHER: Is that it? One measly egg? Every year I make my children a birthday cake. How can I with this? It can't be done! It just can't be done…

MOTHER goes off. The CHICKENS sing nervously.

SONG
The wind it has a bite
It howls all of the night
A shadow hangs upon this land
No hope in the heart of woman or man
Take each day as it comes
Take each day as it comes…

MOTHER comes back with a knife, grabs MAUREEN by the throat and takes her off.

DIANE: Maureen!!!

DIANE goes. FATHER enters and approaches MOTHER.

FATHER: Wife?

MOTHER: Husband?

FATHER: There's only one chicken left.

MOTHER: So long as we keep feeding it

FATHER: But we have no more corn!

MOTHER: Because we cannot afford to buy any.

FATHER: Because I cannot chop down trees.

MOTHER: Because you are too weak.

FATHER: Because there's precious little food. Perhaps Graham has found sustenance in the forest?

(Calls to the wilderness, waits.) Nothing... I hope he comes back soon...

MOTHER: Why would he? There's more chance of survival out there than here!

FATHER: Don't say that wife, please. It's terribly negative.

MOTHER: What are we to do? We have *nothing.*

(Under her breath.)

Oh, swine and bugger and bloody bloody shhh –

FATHER: Please my love, don't swear!

MOTHER: Well, what do you expect me to do? There are too many mouths to feed!

FATHER: Calm... Breathe... There, there... *(An idea.)* Listen, there is one thing we can do that I find always works in times of stress... Hear me out! We could –

(Breaks into gentle song.)

Take each day as it comes...
Take each day as it comes...

MOTHER: What? Not another of your bloody songs? Jacob? Wilhelm? Shut up! Just shut up! Oh, I can't bare this!

She lifts the chopping block high above her head.

FATHER: Wife, what are you doing?

MOTHER: I'm going to knock some bloody sense into you!

MOTHER is about to brain FATHER when...

GRETEL: Mother!

HANSEL: Father!

HANSEL & GRETEL: Today is our birthday.

MOTHER & FATHER: Oh! Yes. Of course!

GRETEL: We're not expecting miracles.

HANSEL: But I would quite like a big slice of cake!

MOTHER & FATHER: Cake? Cake?

MOTHER & FATHER scamper to the back in search of something.

SONG
There is one unique day in every year
When we raise a heartfelt cheer
There's one day we would never cancel
So Happy Birthday, Gretel!
Happy Birthday, Hansel!

The parents reveal "a cake" – a manky potato with a candle in it.

HANSEL: Is that manky potato with a candle in it our birthday cake?

MOTHER: Ingredients were scarce this year, to say the least.

FATHER: Children? You know we would give you the world if we could – but we can't.

MOTHER: Gretel? This morning I went to the edge of the forest and I picked you these lovely marigolds.

GRETEL: They're beautiful. Thanks, Mother.

FATHER: Hansel. This morning I went to the river and I found you these amazing white pebbles!

HANSEL: Oooooh. Thanks... They're great...

HANSEL eats one.

MOTHER & FATHER: Don't eat them, Hansel!

FATHER: Children? Why don't you blow out the candle and make a wish. Perhaps things will turn out for the better!

HANSEL: Oh, I hope so. Let's face it. Things couldn't get much worse.

They go to blow – but a howling famine wind snuffs the candle out before they do. The home is decimated. More crows! More shadows! More hunger! The family are even more despairing – if that's possible.

FATHER: Oh, damn this famine! I will not let it ruin us! Children? Who remembers the family song we used to sing to lift our spirits?

FATHER: Gretel? Do you remember the tune?

GRETEL collapses with hunger.

FATHER: Hansel? Do you remember?

HANSEL: I... I'm... I'm so hungry, father!

HANSEL eats his hat.

FATHER: Wife? Dearest wife, surely you must remember the tune!

MOTHER, hanging off the washing line, appears possessed and freaks FATHER out.

FATHER: *(To himself.)* Come on, man! Think, think... the tune... the tune... the...

(Tries to remember.) The... hills... are aliiiiive with the sound of – "no, that's not right."

GRETEL quietly begins to sing the song.

FATHER: Quiet, darling. Daddy's trying to think...

(Tries again.) Ffffeeed the woooorld – no! That's not right!

GRETEL: *(Sings.)* Yes, we are fine... and we are dandy...

The family stop. It's the song.

GRETEL: Our resolve... with see us through...

(FATHER joins in.)

Yes, we are proud and we are loving...
We're a family good and true!

FATHER: She's got it!

SONG
Yes, we are fine and we are dandy
Our resolve will see us through
Yes, we are proud and we are loving
We're a family good and true

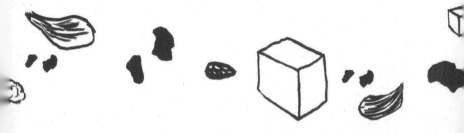

They do the family dance.

SONG
Yes, we are strong and we're resourceful
Though times are often tough
But we'll march through toil and hardship
Of this fight we can't get enough!

MOTHER and FATHER tickle HANSEL & GRETEL to get them out of the way. The song is a momentary reprieve.

MOTHER: Husband?

FATHER: Wife?

MOTHER: Songs are lovely but –

FATHER: I know, I know…

MOTHER: There's not enough food to go around.

FATHER: We're in a tight spot, I confess.

MOTHER: Things are only going to get worse.

FATHER: I don't know what to do, wife!

MOTHER: Something has to be done.

FATHER: Yes. Something. But what?

HANSEL & GRETEL jump on their parents.

SONG
Yes, we are fine and we're dandy
Our resolve will see us through
Yes, we are proud and we are loving
We're a family good and true

HANSEL & GRETEL skip off again.

MOTHER: *(Idea!)* We take Hansel and Gretel into the forest…

FATHER: The forest?

MOTHER: We leave them there.

FATHER: What?

MOTHER: We set them free.

FATHER: Two mouths are easier to feed than four, and we have taught them well.

MOTHER: I say we take them into the forest and we –

MOTHER & FATHER: Let them go!

HANSEL & GRETEL appear again.

SONG
And if one day dark clouds do gather
Should the signs not look so grand
There's our mum and dad to guide us
Cus when we're stuck, they lend a hand

GRETEL overhears this next bit...

FATHER: Wait! There must be some other way!

MOTHER: We have no other choice! Better to survive out there, then to perish here!

FATHER: Our poor, poor children...

MOTHER: Our dear darlings...

MOTHER & FATHER: It's for the best. It's for the best.

SONG *(Big finish.)*
Yes, we are fine and we are dandy
Our resolve will see us through
Yes, we are proud and we are loving
We're a family good and true!!!

HANSEL & GRETEL tickle MOTHER & FATHER.

MOTHER: Hansel? Gretel? Your father and I want to take you in to the forest...

FATHER: For a picnic.

GRETEL: But we have no food.

MOTHER: Then we shall forage!

FATHER: Like Graham! And see what nature's bounty provides! Perhaps we'll find that nice peach tree I'm always going on about. Come along, Hansel. Come along, Gretel.

The parents skip off leaving GRETEL behind.

GRETEL: *(Picking her marigold petals.)* They love us, they love us not… Hansel? Leave a trail.

HANSEL: What?

GRETEL: Drop your pebbles!

HANSEL: Why?

GRETEL: Just do it!

HANSEL & GRETEL leave a trail of petals and pebbles.

FATHER: Come along, Hansel! Come along, Gretel!

They skip until eventually the atmosphere changes…

FATHER: Ah! The forest.

They perform the ancient dance of the Farandol through the forest. Deeper and deeper they go…

FATHER: Ah! Here we are! Hansel? Gretel? Why don't you close your eyes and count backwards from 20. And when you open them… well, you'll have big surprise! Come along now. No peeking.

HANSEL & GRETEL: 20… 19… 18… 17… 16… 15…

The parents, heart-broken, tip-toe off and disappear through the forest.

HANSEL & GRETEL: 6… 5… 4… 321!

They open their eyes.

GRETEL: Father?

HANSEL: Mother? Where is she?

GRETEL: She's probably popped off to forage for nuts and berries. Father?

HANSEL: He's probably gone off to find that peach tree he likes so much!

HANSEL & GRETEL: They'll be back soon. Yes. Back soon…

HANSEL: *(A drowsy fact.)* Gretel, did you know that there are more stars in the sky than there are grains of sand on earth… that's interesting, isn't it?

They fall asleep.

Two RABBITS appear on top of them.

RABBIT 1: I like grass.

RABBIT 2: Me too. It's sweet.

RABBIT 1: Look. Hansel and Gretel have fallen asleep in the deep, dark forest…

RABBIT 2: Oh dear. That's a rather silly thing to do.

RABBIT 1: It's not silly. It's stupid.

RABBIT 2: Stupid.

RABBITS: Stupid! Stupid! Stupid Hansel and Gretel! Stupid, stupid – dumb as a bunch of flowers!

A snare snaps. They freeze. Bud-bud-bud-bud-bud! They vanish. HANSEL & GRETEL wake with a start.

GRETEL: Mother?

HANSEL: Father!

GRETEL: It's dark.

HANSEL: It's night! How do we find our way home?

GRETEL: The petals!

HANSEL: The pebbles!

HANSEL & GRETEL: The petals and the pebbles!

They look for them but…

HANSEL & GRETEL: It's too dark to see!

They wander through the forest – it's dark and scary.

SONG
Forest of fish bone
Forest of apple core
Forest of egg shells
Forest of wanting more
Forest of empty plate
Forest of cupboards bare
Forest of bread crumbs
Forest of nothing there

Suddenly, from the shadows, a strange, cackling character appears on an old bicycle. She shoots fire out of her fingertips and brings knives hurtling out of the sky.

HANSEL & GRETEL are frightened and run.

SONG
Forest of weariness
Forest of growing doubt
Forest of getting lost
Forest of without
Forest of watchful eyes
Forest of bated breath
Forest of broken teeth
Forest of hovering death

The stranger carries on into the woods.

The moon rises, revealing the pebbles and petals in its light.

GRETEL: Hansel, there's our way home!

HANSEL: Come on!

They start to follow the trail back. Suddenly, the strange character appears again – this time with a leaf-blower. She blasts the petals they've passed over, obliterating the trail home.

The strange character comes to a stop, sniffs the wind, and catches a rabbit by the neck with a snare-crack!

STRANGE CHARACTER: Haha! Got ya!

(Sings.)

Old Mary's gone a-hunting
She'll never be a bride
Old Mary's gone a-hunting
The world had better hide!

She skips off into the darkness.

Home.

DIANE sits alone in the wasteland.

DIANE: Things have gone from bad to worse, haven't they Maureen? Maureen? Oh. I forgot.

(Sings.)

Maureen, my hen
You were my friend
The world's not been right
Since you met your swift end

So tell me Maureen
Is there life after death?
Or does consciousness stop
With your very last breath?

Goodbye Maureen, goodbye…
Goodbye Maureen, goodbye…
Goodbye Maureen, goodbye…
Goodbye Maureen, goodbye…

MOTHER appears. She checks the bird for eggs.

MOTHER: Nothing… Not one egg! We have nothing! Oh…
Oh, look! A worm!

Both MOTHER & DIANE go for it. MOTHER wins, and boots DIANE off.

MOTHER: It's my worm! Mine!

She eats it.

MOTHER: Oh, that's so succulent and juicy!

Then begins to sing.

SONG
Life is hard
And flinty-sharp
With pickings slim
I hate to carp
I used to be
A woman proud
But I just ate a worm
From out of the ground!

CHORUS
Something must be done
Something must be done
This madness can't go on…

(She sings alone.)

The floor is dirt
The sky is grey
I'm on my knees
I hope and pray
The cupboard's bare

No wood, no coal
And my stomach's
An empty hole!

CHORUS
Ohhhh!
Something must be done
Something must be done
No, this madness can't go on!

MOTHER wails to the heavens. FATHER, who's been attempting to chop a small piece of wood but hasn't the strength, notices her.

FATHER: Wife? What are you doing?

MOTHER: Nothing, husband.

FATHER: Then, why all the wailing?

MOTHER: Husband, I just ate a worm.

FATHER: A worm?

MOTHER: A worm from out of the ground. Oh, what have I done? What have I become?

FATHER: Oh, my dear, it's all right. It's all right.

MOTHER: I miss our children.

FATHER: I know you do, my dear, but what's done is done…
Two mouths are easier to feed than four.

MOTHER & FATHER do a slow, sad dance. HANSEL & GRETEL return. MOTHER & FATHER can't believe their eyes.

SONG *(A tender reprise.)*
Yes we are fine and we are dandy
Our resolve will see us through
Yes we are proud and we are loving
We're a family good and true…

FATHER: Our children…

MOTHER: Our children have come home.

FATHER: Let's eat!

MOTHER: But we have nothing…

DIANE clucks, off. MOTHER has an idea. She chases DIANE with an axe – THUNK!

HANSEL eyes FATHER warily.

FATHER: *(Ashamed, offering hand.)* Hansel?

They play a round of Thumb War – this time HANSEL properly wins.

HANSEL: Oh father, you are weak.

FATHER: And you, Hansel, are almost a man.

MOTHER: Dinner's ready! Here… you children should eat it.

HANSEL & GRETEL are encouraged to eat the chicken as MOTHER & FATHER watch on, starving.

FATHER: Two mouths are easier to feed than four… Soon we will be gone…

MOTHER: Cast to the four winds…

FATHER: Nothing but dust on the empty breeze…

MOTHER: There is nothing to be done… Nothing to be done…

HANSEL: *(Holding a plate of chicken bones.)* Mother? Father? I'm still hungry…

FATHER: Oh, Hansel.

FATHER spots a mouse.

FATHER: Wife. Children. Look! It's a mouse.

FATHER tries to catch it but he's too slow. The mouse darts down a hole. The family despair.

MOTHER: How could you let him slip through your fingers? He was good enough to eat!

GRETEL: *(Idea!)* Good enough to eat… Hansel, come on!

GRETEL springs into action.

MOTHER: Oh, I'm so hungry it hurts!

FATHER: It's alright, dear, I'll find you something.

(Finds chicken feathers.)

Wife? Take this chicken feather! Suck the nutrients out of the ruddy thing!

(They suck feathers loudly.)

GRETEL: *(Up high, rigging things.)* Mother? Father? I've got an idea! A new invention!

FATHER: You be careful up there, Gretel!

GRETEL: Don't you worry about me, father.

MOTHER: *(To us.)* All I ever wanted was a safe home for them. With a roof over their heads, and food on the table.

GRETEL swings off a rope which lifts a huge slab of tree. She works fast and light, creating the device with HANSEL's help.

MOTHER: It's not as easy as it looks – the raising of children.

With all of his might, HANSEL pulls two lengths of rope and connects them.

FATHER: Oh, that's it my boy. Be strong! Oh, look at him! He's like an ox!

MOTHER: *(It's hard.)* Teaching them what's right. Knowing what's wrong. When sometimes it's difficult to know yourself. You see, there were no clear instructions that came with you two marvellous inventions. We just did what we thought was best.

GRETEL: Hansel? Light the lamp.

HANSEL strikes a match, lights the lamp screwed to an old plank, which sits on a seesaw-like pivot.

GRETEL: Mother? Father? Behold! The Mouse Trap!

EVERYONE: Oooh.

GRETEL: Stand back. Now, where's that mouse…?

HANSEL: There he is!

Indeed, the mouse has popped up in another place, and sits directly beneath the huge hanging log. Its tail hooks a nail and starts a chain reaction, releasing a ball which rolls into a sprung trigger, which fires a cannonball through the air and into a bucket which tips the plank which brings the flame up to a taut, rigged rope… which it slowly burns through until – SNAP! The suspended log drops. BAM! The mouse is squashed flat. Everyone cheers.

FATHER: Gretel, you clever sausage!

GRETEL: Here, mother. Here, father. This is for you.

FATHER: Wife? Let's eat!

MOTHER & FATHER take the mouse, and devour it.

HANSEL: Gretel, we can't go on like this.

GRETEL: Hansel, one mouse will never be enough.

HANSEL & GRETEL: We have to do something.

SONG
There's warmth in the wilderness
There's embrace in the dark
There's light from the half moon

43

There's night's beating heart
There's caress in the brambles
There's hush on the wind
There's "sleep tight" in the wolf's cry
The shadows, your friend
The shadows, your friend

You've well earned the right
You've held in there tight
Tonight is your night of rest
You need not take flight
From this daunting night
Tonight is your night of rest

HANSEL: We have to help them.

GRETEL: And ourselves.

HANSEL: But what can we do? We're only children.

GRETEL: Hansel, we have to leave.

They don balaclavas, gather their things, put blankets on MOTHER & FATHER.

HANSEL: Two mouths are easier to feed than four.

They are about to leave when –

WILHELM: Hansel. Gretel. Take the very last of our bread.

JACOB: We baked it ourselves.

They take the bread.

HANSEL: Thank you, Wilhelm.

GRETEL: Thank you, Jacob.

JACOB: Good luck.

WILHELM: Good luck.

HANSEL & GRETEL STARE AT JACOB AND WILHELM.

WILHELM/JACOB: Well go on, then.

HANSEL & GRETEL are ready for the wilderness. They hold the bread aloft.

GRETEL: Do we eat to survive?

HANSEL: Or leave a trail home instead?

GRETEL: The world is hungrier than we are!

HANSEL: Let's cast it to the four winds!

HANSEL & GRETEL crumble the bread as they go and throw it up to the sky. It starts to snow. They enter the forest.

HANSEL & GRETEL replace themselves with their wooden dolls – two miniature versions of themselves in the wilderness.

SONG
There's shelter in the dread cave
There's comfort in the storm
There's blankets under dead leaves
There's kindness in thorns

There's sweet song in the frog croak
There's sign-posts in the mist
The dew that falls upon you
Is a sweet goodnight kiss
It's a sweet goodnight kiss

You've well earned the right
You've held in there tight
Tonight is your night of rest
You need not take flight
From this daunting night

Tonight is your night of rest

But tomorrow
Tomorrow brings the test…

Above, a miniature house made of bread floats in – a tiny bird circles it. An inviting light glows within. The strange character from before looks down from on high at the tiny wooden HANSEL & GRETEL dolls.

STRANGE CHARACTER: Yes… Tomorrow brings the test!

The sound of a thousand birds descending.

ACT TWO

The sound of a thousand birds flying off. HANSEL & GRETEL wake up.

GRETEL: I had a dream…

HANSEL: Of freshly baked bread…

GRETEL: And we ate and ate and ate!

HANSEL: Until our empty bellies were fed!

GRETEL: But there isn't any.

HANSEL: No. It's gone. Every crumb.

Suddenly, a BIRD appears and calls to them.

BIRD: Follow! Follow! Follow me!

GRETEL: What a strange bird.

HANSEL: I've never seen a bird like that before. I wonder what species it is.

BIRD: Follow! Follow meeee!

HANSEL: If only we could understand its strange song…

BIRD: Thissa way! Thissa way!

HANSEL: It's almost as if it's trying to say something.

BIRD: Yoooou twoooo – follow me!

(Spelling it out.) Follow *me*!

GRETEL: I think she wants us to follow her.

BIRD: Bingo!

The BIRD takes flight and leads them to…

A house made of bread.

GRETEL: The smell of fresh baked bread! It's coming from that house!

HANSEL: It's not coming *from* the house. It *is* the house.

BIRD: Stuff yourselves! Go on! Gobble! Gobble! Gobble! Gobble! Tweet – eat – eat eat!

GRETEL: Hungry…

HANSEL: So hungry…

GRETEL: Should we?

HANSEL: We should.

Famished, they pull handfuls of bread from the roof and eat.

HANSEL: An incredible, edible house! What luck!

GRETEL: It's the house of our dreams!

VOICE: *(From within.)* Nibbledydee, niddlebyday! Who's that nibbling at my house today?

They stop – and call into the house.

HANSEL: Tis but the wind!

GRETEL: Yes. The wind!

HANSEL: The whispering friend!

VOICE: The wind?

The bread door slowly starts to open and reveals

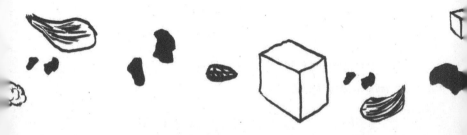

A LITTLE OLD LADY. She dresses like Fanny Craddock and wears dark glasses. She sniffs the air. HANSEL & GRETEL hide, mouths stuffed with bread.

OLD LADY: Children? Is that the sweet smell of children?

The BIRD lands on her outstretched arm. It squawks at HANSEL & GRETEL.

OLD LADY: Oh, forgive me my dears, my eyes are dim. Here. Let me feel you both.

(Feels them.)

Oh! There's nothing to you. You're skin and bone! I see now what you mean – you're *thin* as wind! You must be *hungry*. Shoo!

The BIRD flies into the house.

OLD LADY: Why don't you stop eating my house, eh?

HANSEL: Oh. We've been eating her house.

GRETEL: Oh. I've been eating the chimney.

OLD LADY: You have! You have… Poor pickles, skinny as sticks! Why don't you come inside. I'll cook you something delicious. Come in. Come in!

HANSEL & GRETEL can't believe their luck, and step inside the house.

OLD LADY: Oh, children!

The OLD LADY smiles sweetly as she closes the door with a creak and a slam.

Inside.

OLD LADY: Welcome!

The BIRD sits on a perch and screeches.

OLD LADY: Calm yourself, Birdy! We have guests. This is Birdy! She's a Canadian Peekaboo Owl Hawk, don't you know? They're renowned for their extreme swings in emotion.

BIRDY runs a gamut of emotions.

OLD LADY: Now. Who's hungry?

HANSEL: I am!

GRETEL: We are!

HANSEL: Starving!

GRETEL: Ravenous!

HANSEL: Look at us!

GRETEL: Look at us!

OLD LADY: Let me feel your spindly frames once more!

HANSEL: Our stomachs are as deep as bottomless wells!

GRETEL: Shout down my throat, you'll hear it echo!

OLD LADY: Hello?

It echoes.

OLD LADY: Now, howbout Rabbit stew?

HANSEL & GRETEL: *(Echoing.)* Rabbit stew! Rabbit stew! Stew! Stew! Stew!

OLD LADY: I pity the cry of poor, famished beasts!
Now, where's my apron! Let's cook up a feast!

Music plays as the OLD LADY skips into action. BIRDY prepares the table.

BIRDY: Siddown! Siddown!

HANSEL & GRETEL sit.

OLD LADY: Now I've just the cure for rumbling tums
Like shortcake biscuits and sugar plums
What are you hungry for? What's your desire?
Once you've tasted you'll never tire

Of my fabulous gooey banana sponge
Or my legendary dish, *duck a la orange*?

The OLD LADY and BIRDY prepare the dishes through increasingly bizarre mime.

OLD LADY: Howbout roast chicken with crisp golden spuds?
Followed by pudding with cream by the tub?

The OLD LADY and BIRDY dance and make a tower of pancakes.

HANSEL: Gretel, sister – we've come up trumps!

GRETEL: We've struck gold, brother! Gold!

HANSEL: She's the best cook in all the land!

GRETEL: Perhaps even the world!

HANSEL: She's so kind!

GRETEL: So generous!

HANSEL: So friendly!

GRETEL: Such a warm-hearted woman!

HANSEL: Can we can you "auntie"?

OLD LADY: Oh! Yes! Of course! Auntie!

Take your fill, sweethearts! Stuff your dear faces!
"Ping!" go your buttons and "pop!" Go your braces!

Whatever you crave, I can provide the lot!
There's endless deliciousness comes from my pot!

Ladels of scrumptious! Spoonfuls of yum!
The meals I'll make, they'll be better than mum's!

GRETEL: *(Suddenly stopping.)* Mother?

HANSEL: Father?

GRETEL: I wish they were here.

HANSEL: I miss them.

GRETEL: I miss home.

HANSEL: Home…

OLD LADY: It's all here for you to be chewed and digested –
Eat til you burst! Let not one crumb go wasted!

*The OLD LADY & BIRDY dance, then set about feeding HANSEL &
GRETEL to bursting. They eat and eat and eat (again, mimed) until
there is nothing left.*

HANSEL: I never thought… I'd say this but… I'm full up…

GRETEL: I never thought… I'd say this but… I really couldn't
eat… another… thing…

HANSEL: I know… what you mean, sister… I know…what…
you…

The OLD LADY & BIRDY lay a blanket on top of them.

OLD LADY: Hush now… Hush now… Hush now…
Sleep, children. Sleep.

BIRDY: Sleep… perchance to dream…

OLD LADY: Birdy? Mummy's orf a-hunting.

She skips off.

BIRDY: Fall asleep children
Hide in your dreams,
Things in the flesh
Aren't quite what they seem…

*The OLD LADY appears with her bike, dressed up in her hunting
gear – this is the strange character we saw earlier!*

OLD LADY: Night hangs open like a dead man's yawn!
I shall plague the earth! I shall hunt 'til dawn!

BIRDY: *(Circling, swooping, diving.)* The Witching Hour is upon
us! Take flight, children! Oh, take thy flight! Or you might
not survive this terrible night!

The OLD LADY flies on her bike and hunts the forest.

OLD LADY: *(A sinister ditty.)*
Old Mary's gone a-hunting
She'll never be a bride
Old Mary's gone a-hunting
The world had better hide

She catches a rabbit with the same terrible snare-crack we've heard before.

OLD LADY: Got ya!

(Sings.)

Old Mary's gone a-hunting
She'll never be a bride
Old Mary's gone a –

A hissing sound. The hunting comes to a stand-still.

OLD LADY: Oh no. Bloody puncture!

Back to the bread house – it starts to transform into a place of nightmare…

Children's shoes and bones. Old teddy bears fall from the roof and come to life, crawling all over the sleeping HANSEL & GRETEL.

BIRDY sings:

SONG
Run away children
Hide in your dreams

Things in the flesh
Aren't quite what they seem!

Morning.

HANSEL & GRETEL wake up. Teddy bears are scattered about the place.

HANSEL: I had the strangest dreams.

GRETEL: As did I, brother.

BIRDY: Well, what do you expect, going to bed on a full stomach?

HANSEL: What?

BIRDY: Ca-caw!

Enter OLD LADY.

OLD LADY: Morning, little buttons! Now, what would you two clamoring chicks like for breakfast? Howbout rabbitrabbitrabbit?

She holds up a brace of dead rabbits.

GRETEL: I'm not hungry, thank you.

HANSEL: Yes. I'm still full.

OLD LADY: But a hearty appetite means a healthy soul!

The OLD LADY hangs the rabbits.

HANSEL: Perhaps we could have a spot of breakfast, eh Gretel? What's on the menu today, auntie?

OLD LADY: Oh. Why Hansel, *you* are.

An ominous moment.

GRETEL: What?

OLD LADY: You're sitting on it.

HANSEL: Oh. Ha! For a moment there I thought you meant *I* was on the menu!

They laugh nervously. GRETEL finds a pair of children's shoes hanging.

GRETEL: Whose little shoes are these, Auntie?

OLD LADY: Oh… A wandering child… such as yourself left them here once… they soon had no use for them.

Another ominous moment.

GRETEL: Why?

OLD LADY: She was a pretty young girl who loved to drink milk by the gallon! Soon her feet became as big as cheeses! Ha!

HANSEL & GRETEL laugh nervously.

GRETEL: Then, what of this pair?

OLD LADY: A lost boy found his way to the house once. He ate so much fruit that his feet swelled to the size of sweet juicy watermelons!

They laugh nervously. They see shoes hanging everywhere.

GRETEL: And what about all those?

OLD LADY: All those what?

GRETEL: All those shoes.

OLD LADY: What shoes?

GRETEL: And all these teddy bears?

OLD LADY: What teddy bears?

GRETEL: And all these *bones*!

OLD LADY: I see no bones.

GRETEL: That's because you're blind!

OLD LADY: Oh!

HANSEL: Gretel!

GRETEL: Well she is!

OLD LADY: Yes! It is true! My eyes are dim. But Birdy, my
feathery friend, sees all. Birdy?

BIRDY: *(Landing on her arm.)* Caw?

OLD LADY: Be mummy's eyes!

BIRDY: I'll be mummy's eyes!

HANSEL: Auntie? We'd like to go home now.

OLD LADY: Go home, dears? Why? Whatever for?
What's there to go home to? Stay… We can eat. And eat.
And eat…

The brace of dead rabbits come to life and moan.

DEAD RABBITS
Run away children
Hide in your dreams
Things in the flesh
Aren't quite what they seem!

GRETEL: Auntie? I accuse you of being… a witch!

The OLD LADY chuckles and then transforms into a WITCH!

*Her dress peels off like dead skin to reveal a saggy, bloated, moldy,
bald monster.*

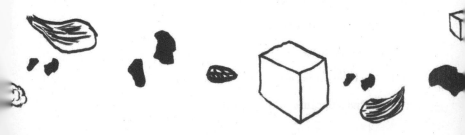

56

BIRDY: Yes! She is a witch, as it's plain to see!
   Now which one will the witch have for her tea?

WITCH: Yes! Which one's the most succulent? The most falls-off-the-bone? The most melts-in-the-mouth? They're all tough skin and chewy flesh – but I must make my choice over which one to cook first! Now which one will it be?

   (Pause.)

   Birdy? Put the boy in the cage.

HANSEL: You will never get me in that cage, you hag!

WITCH: Get in the cage, boy!

   The WITCH uses her magical powers to get him into the cage.

HANSEL: My… legs…!

   HANSEL is crammed into a small cage, then hoisted high.

GRETEL: Leave my brother alone!

   GRETEL bites THE WITCH.

WITCH: Oww! Sit down you little brat!

   The WITCH uses magic to tie GRETEL to a chair. It should be impressive – and mimed.

WITCH: Yes! Yes! Yes!

   She takes a bow – which must provoke a round of applause to enable the next line –

WITCH: *(To audience.)* Oh, thank you for applauding cannibalism. Now, Hansel, m'boy? I am going to hang you there and I am going to feed you until you are perfectly plump. Then I shall stack the wood high, suspend you over the flames and cook you until you are tender… and then, little man, I shall gobble you up! Oh, I shall gobble you up!

   The WITCH exits.

HANSEL: Oh, Gretel. What are we going to do?

GRETEL: Don't worry, brother. I'll think of something.

Forest.

Two RABBITS pop up shaking with fear.

RABBIT 1: Let's sing songs to forget the horrors of what we've just seen.

RABBIT 2: Yes, good idea.

RABBITS: "Everything is beautiful…"

RABBIT 1: "Rain drops and roses…"

RABBIT 2: "Bright eyes, burning like fire…"

RABBIT 1: Don't sing that!

RABBIT 2: Oh no! It's a horrible song! Stupid! Stupid! Poor Hansel. It looks like his days are numbered.

RABBIT 1: Well, it's a wonder we're still here.

RABBIT 2: We'll always be here. We're survivors.

RABBIT 1: Yes, you won't get rid of us so easily.

RABBIT 2: Thank heavens for "proliferation", that's what I say.

RABBIT 1: That's a big word.

RABBIT 2: I know. It means we are voracious procreators and propagate our species at an exponential rate.

RABBIT 1 stares blankly, then:

RABBIT 1: I like grass.

A snare goes off. Bud-bud-bud… they scarper.

Back to the house.

HANSEL hangs in a cage, eating and eating.

HANSEL: *(Sings.)*
I wish I could stop eating
But it's going down a treat

I'll soon be fat enough to cook
And good enough to eat...

(Spoken.)

Oh, Gretel, this is torture!

GRETEL: Hansel! Stop eating! She's plumping you up like the Christmas turkey!

HANSEL: But it tastes so good! I can't resist! I've got toasted bread. The finest smoked cheese. Cold-cut meats. Dollops of jam. Lashings of cream.

GRETEL: Oooooooh.

Enter WITCH.

WITCH: How's the eating going Hansel? Keeping eating, boy! Keep eating!

Stuffing his face with more food.

GRETEL: Hansel!

WITCH: All you'll get is crab shell soup, girl, but only after you've finished your tasks for the day, the first of which is to fix the puncture on my bicycle.

BIRDY wheels the broken bike in.

GRETEL: I can't work if I'm tied up.

WITCH: *(To audience.)* Saucy minx, isn't she? Don't try anything clever...

With magic, the rope comes undone.

WITCH: Now go. Fix the tire.

GRETEL attends to the wheel, pumping up the tire up.

WITCH: And after that be sure you grease the chain, and after that you can chop the kindling for the fire, and after that you can water my vegetable patch, pick some potatoes for the pot and peel 'em perfectly!

(Sings.)

Poor Iris loved a sailor
She wept as he departed
He swore he'd find his way home
To finish what he started

(To HANSEL.)

Keep eating, boy. Oh, what a feast you will be!

(Sings.)

But the sailor had no compass
And so no path was charted
Poor Iris waits for him
Upon the shore all broken-hearted

(Spoken.)

Birdy? Be mummy's eyes.

WITCH exits.

BIRDY watches HANSEL & GRETEL.

HANSEL: Sister? I don't want to be eaten.

GRETEL: I know you don't, brother.

HANSEL: I'm a young man, not a morsel of food. Those lessons father gave will be for nothing. There must be a way to break me free!

GRETEL: I'm working on it, brother.

HANSEL: What will become of me? I'm destined for the witch's belly, and the never-ending void that is her churning, gurgling guts. There is… no hope.

(Suddenly brightening.)

Oh, look! A fruit bun!

He scoffs it.

BIRDY watches from her perch, and reflects.

BIRDY: Oh, those poor children, trapped against their will, longing for home.

(She remembers.)

"Home". *Canada.* Oh, sweet, sweet Canada. How I miss thy mighty cloud-kissing mountain peaks. How I yearn to skim the endless glassy lakes of Winnipeg once again! But alas, my wings are clipped and my soul is tethered to the witch's wicked wrist. You see, I wasn't always called Birdy. My true Canadian Peekaboo Hawk Owl name is Tuk-tay-ak-took! Which, roughly translated means, "She Who Dances Alone For Long Periods Of Time." Oh, Canada. Oh, sweet, sweet Canada!

(To audience.)

Please stand for the Canadian national anthem.

(Sings.)

Oh, Canada, we stand on guard for thee
Oh, Canada, we stand on guard for thee

(To audience.)

Everybody!

(Sings.)

Oh, Canada, we stand on guard for thee!

(Note: The part of BIRDY is tailored to the actor's actual nationality. In the first version of the show, the bird was called Hamlet, and was a Bolivian Condor. Don't ask.)

BIRDY bows and returns to her perch.

GRETEL chops wood with a big axe.

HANSEL: I want to go home, Gretel.

GRETEL: I know you do, brother. I wonder what mother and father are doing?

HANSEL & GRETEL: *(Sing.)*
Yes we are fine and we are dandy...

Enter the WITCH. She is sickened by the cute song.

GRETEL: I've just watered your vegetable patch.

WITCH: Good. And I hope you peeled the spuds! I like a bit of veg with my meat. Is the fire prepared?

GRETEL: Yes.

WITCH: Good! Now. Who's hungry?

HANSEL: Not me.

GRETEL: Nor me.

BIRDY: Caw! Or me!

WITCH: Well I am! I am horribly starved. So. Let's get cooking!

She lights the fire.

WITCH: I shall let the flames rage and roar until the heat is just right! After all Hansel I want to cook you, not burn you. Tell me boy – are you plump enough yet? Are you suitably roastable?

HANSEL: No, Witch. I am but a bag o' bones and will surely taste of the foulest meat should you cook me.

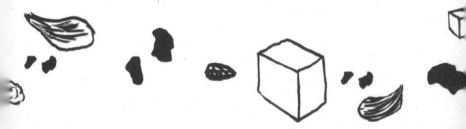

WITCH: Is that so? Why don't you poke your finger through the bars so that I might judge for myself just how perfectly plump you are.

HANSEL: My finger?

WITCH: Your digit, your pinky, your pointer, I want it – now!

HANSEL: *(Thinking fast.)* Before I do, witch... did you know that the smallest bone –

WITCH: Bone? Bone? What bone?

HANSEL: *(To GRETEL.)* The smallest *bone* – the smallest bone in the human body is located in the ear?

GRETEL gets the message and picks up a large bone.

WITCH: No. I didn't know that.

HANSEL: And did you also know, Witch, that in Mediaeval times, people were much smaller –

(To GRETEL.)

Much *smaller* –

WITCH: Smaller?

HANSEL: Yes, *much smaller* than they are today on account of their vitamin-deprived diet!

GRETEL gets the message and finds a smaller bone. Shows it to HANSEL. It isn't right.

WITCH: That's all very interesting, boy. However –

HANSEL: And did you also know, Witch, that the Egyptian scorpion can kill two horses with a single sting of its tail even though it's only…

(To GRETEL.)

the size of a finger!

WITCH: The size of a finger, you say?

HANSEL: Yes, the size of a *finger*!

GRETEL gets the message and offers a finger-sized bone…

WITCH: Which reminds me… Finger!

But the WITCH is in the way and she can't get it to HANSEL.

BIRDY: Oh, these poor innocent children. I can stand idly by no longer! I must help them!

WITCH: Finger, I say!

BIRDY: Witch, did you know that the average lead pencil can draw a line that is almost 35 miles long?

WITCH: Don't you start, Birdy!

GRETEL scampers by the WITCH undetected.

BIRDY: It's true! Of course, it's all to do with the type of lead in the pencil – 2B… or not 2B, that is the question!

WITCH: Birdy! Shoo! Now… for the last time, boy – finger!

GRETEL gets the bone to HANSEL in the nick of time.

HANSEL: Very well. Here, Witch.

He sticks the bone out. The WITCH finds and feels it thoroughly.

WITCH: Damn and blast! You *are* still thin. Keep eating, boy! Keep eating!

HANSEL: I can't eat any more!

WITCH: Oh, my boy... There's always room for more...
Now EAT!

Behind her, GRETEL, in collusion with BIRDY, finishes off her ultimate contraption using watering cans, the kindling axe, the bicycle, etc.

WITCH: A child's flesh I'll have for tea
It is my favorite recipe
Add a pinch of foreign spice
That makes a little boy taste nice
Boiling blood and crunchy spine
Every scrap is so divine!

CHORUS
Stoke the flames and carve the meat!
A little boy tastes oh so sweet!
Stoke the flames! And carve the meat!
A little boy tastes oh so sweet!

Now, dance!

WITCH makes everyone dance with her magic.

WITCH: Rub this salt into your skin.

HANSEL: Why?

WITCH: Season yourself.

HANSEL: I don't want to season myself!

WITCH: And pop these behind your ears, there's a good fellow.

HANSEL: What are they?

WITCH: Sprigs of rosemary.

HANSEL: No!

WITCH: And smear yourself in this!

HANSEL: What is it?

WITCH: Butter brandy Marinade!

HANSEL: I won't!

WITCH: Insolent little morsel!

Magic! HANSEL sprinkles salt and brushes himself with sauce.

HANSEL: I hope I make you sick!

WITCH: Finger!

HANSEL pokes out the chicken bone. WITCH feels.

WITCH: Still no plumper! Eat, boy! Eat!

HANSEL: Oh, Gretel! Help me!

CHORUS
Stoke the flames and carve the meat
A little boy tastes oh so sweet!
Stoke the flames and carve the meat
A little boy tastes oh so sweet!

WITCH: Auntie's getting ready for dinner!

She removes her apron and starts to dance, flames shooting from her fingers!

WITCH: Gut the carcase like a fish
Crack the wishbone! Make a wish!
Rub some salt and score the flesh
When buying boy make sure it's fresh
The calories are quite obscene
Oh, blow the diet – add some cream!

Picture this lump on a plate
It makes me want to salivate
Coals are hot, the knife is sharp
This is my very favorite part
This brat will turn out like a dream
Crank up the heat – Gas Mark 13!!!

Flames roar from the fire-pit as the WITCH leads the dance to its grotesque finale.

WITCH: *(To HANSEL.)* Finger!

HANSEL: Witch, did you know that the North European Hawk Moth looks just like a –

WITCH: Finger?

HANSEL: And did you know that Sir Isaac Newton discovered gravity when an apple fell on his –

WITCH: Finger!

HANSEL: And did you know that the biggest Californian Redwood ever recorded was as tall as a –

WITCH: FINGER.

HANSEL pokes the chicken bone out. She grasps the bone, snatching it clean out of his hand.

HANSEL: Oh, no!

WITCH: What…?

She feels both ends of the bone, realises she's been duped, and snaps it in two.

WITCH: You tricked me with a bone, you naughty… little… boy. Give me your real finger!

She reaches into the cage and feels his real finger.

WITCH: Ah ha! I knew it! Oh Hansel! You… are… fat!

HANSEL: No!

GRETEL is about to activate the contraption.

GRETEL: Don't worry, Hansel –

WITCH: Sit down!

The WITCH magics GRETEL into the chair and ties her up.

GRETEL: No!

WITCH: *(To audience.)* The fire is ready.

HANSEL: Gretel! Help!

WITCH: All that remains is for me to season the white-hot coals with finest herbs...

HANSEL: Gretel, whatever you've been planning –

WITCH: And then we cook the boy!

HANSEL: Now's the time to do it!

GRETEL: It's now or never!

While the WITCH turns her back to scatter the herbs onto the fire, GRETEL, tied to the chair, hops with all her might in an attempt to activate the contraption.

WITCH: What's that noise? What are you up to, child? Stop shuffling about!

GRETEL hops in the chair again – the watering can drops and starts to fill a bucket with water...

WITCH: I said stop –

(Hears the water filling the bucket.)

Who's watering my vegetable patch?

The bucket drops, the chain reaction begins...

WITCH: *(Staggering blindly about the place.)* What's that? What's going on? Birdy? These brats are up to no good! Birdy, be mummy's eyes! Birdy? Where are you? We must cook the boy now!

BIRDY: Be your own eyes, witch!

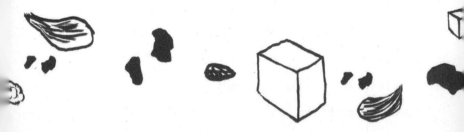

68

The axe suddenly falls and releases HANSEL and the cage. He swings wildly through the air just as the WITCH gropes for him.

WITCH: Where is he? Hansel? Auntie's coming for you… and when she gets you… she's going to cook you!

A series of close shaves and near-misses as the cage cuts through the air like a deadly pendulum!

WITCH: Where are you?

HANSEL: I'm *HERE!*

HANSEL's cage slams into the WITCH. She is knocked into the flames. Her screams in agony and sinks into the red-hot glow. HANSEL is released. Everyone sighs with relief.

GRETEL: She's dead.

Suddenly, THE WITCH BURSTS OUT OF THE FLAMES, SHRIEKING AND ABLAZE! KAMIKAZE RABBITS leap out of nowhere and go for the WITCH's throat.

RABBITS: Revenge! Revenge! Revenge is sweet!

She falls back into the smoke and flames. Sigh of relief.

GRETEL: She really is dead.

The WITCH BURSTS OUT AGAIN – THIS TIME A SMOULDERING SKELETON WHICH SCREAMS, THEN EXPLODES INTO A SHOWER OF DUST. Sigh of relief.

BIRDY: That has it to be it, surely? The Witch is Dead?

Beat.

The Witch is Dead!

Everyone cheers.

BIRDY: My friends, can you smell that? Can you smell the smell of freedom? Can you taste the taste? We are free! Free to return home! Goodbye my friends! And thank you.

(Sings.)

Oh Canada!

She sings as she goes, then appears in the distance, a small BIRD flying high.

BIRDY: Look in the cellar! Look in the cellar! The cellar…

BIRDY disappears.

HANSEL & GRETEL: The cellar?

HANSEL & GRETEL see a trap door in the floor and prise it up to reveal food in abundance.

HANSEL: Look! There's fruit!

GRETEL: And corn!

HANSEL: And bread!

GRETEL: There's more than anyone could ever want!

HANSEL: More than anyone could ever wish for!

GRETEL: Let's go home.

HANSEL: Home.

They collect it all up in a cart and make the journey home.

SONG
There's warmth in the wilderness
There's embrace in the dark
There's light from the half moon
There's night's beating heart
There's caress in the brambles
There's hush on the wind
There's "sleep tight" in the wolf's cry
The shadows, your friend
The shadows, your friend

You've well earned the right
You've held in there tight
Tonight is your night of rest
You need not take flight

From this daunting night
Tonight is your night of rest
HANSEL & GRETEL lay a trail of teddy bears and shoes as they
wind their way back through the forest.

SONG
There's shelter in the dread cave
There's comfort in the storm
There's blankets under dead leaves
There's kindness in thorns
There's sweet song in the frog croak
There's sign-posts in the mist
The dew that falls upon you
Is a sweet goodnight kiss
It's a sweet goodnight kiss

You've well earned the right
You've held in there tight
Tonight is your night of rest
You need not take flight
From this daunting night
Tonight is your night of rest

RABBITS watch them.

RABBIT 1: Not so stupid after all, eh?

RABBIT 2: I like grass.

RABBIT 1: Me too. It's sweet.

RABBIT 2: And oh so green.

RABBIT 1: I feel brave today.

RABBIT 2: And so do I.

The RABBITS hop with a new-found confidence. One hops on top of the other, but the light fades on them before anything too graphic is seen.

Back home.

HANSEL & GRETEL make a shrine of food. MOTHER and FATHER appear in rags, and can't believe their eyes. GRETEL hands MOTHER an apple. She takes a bite.

FATHER: Our children.

MOTHER: Our children have come home!

The family are re-united. MOTHER hugs GRETEL. FATHER & HANSEL play Thumb War, but do away with it.

Music drifts in…

HANSEL: Hark!

MOTHER: Is that Jacob?

FATHER: And Wilhelm?

GRETEL: Our musical neighbours from across the valley!

JACOB & WILHELM appear, yodelling. The family join in.

GRETEL: Make yourselves at home, boys.

JACOB: Thank you.

WILHELM: Thank you.

GRETEL: The forest doesn't look so big anymore.

HANSEL: I wonder what lies beyond it?

GRETEL: Let's find out…

HANSEL & GRETEL: Tomorrow.

HANSEL: *(Twitching and dancing in his laderhosen.)* Oh!

GRETEL: What is it?

HANSEL: I don't know, I – Oh!

HANSEL finds a ferret in his trousers.

HANSEL: I've got my very own ferret down my trousers!

Everyone cheers.

SONG
Once upon a time
When stories were written in rhyme
And winter melted into spring
The folk of those days were known to sing
Take each day as it comes
Take each day as it comes
Take each day as it comes
Take each day as it comes…

The band leads out a procession of celebration.

THE END.